REASONS TO
PERSIST

ALSO BY FRANCES BRADLEY ROBINSON
From Stressed to Blessed: A Personal Journey
ISBN 978-1-947506-00-8

REASONS TO PERSIST

A Biography of Isaac Franklin Bradley

FRANCES BRADLEY ROBINSON

LaunchCrate Publishing
Kansas City

Copyright 2018 © by LaunchCrate Publishing &
Frances Bradley Robinson

All rights reserved. No part of this publication may be reproduced, distributed, or transmitted in any form or by any means, including photocopying, recording, or other electronic or mechanical methods, without the prior written permission of the publisher, except in the case of brief quotations embodied in critical reviews and certain other noncommercial uses permitted by copyright law. For permission requests, email the publisher with subject "Attention: Permissions Coordinator," at the address below.

LaunchCrate Publishing
info@launchcrate.com
www.launchcrate.com

Ordering Information:
Quantity sales. Special discounts are available on quantity purchases by corporations, associations, and others. For details, contact the publisher at the email address above. Orders by U.S. trade bookstores and wholesalers.

Library of Congress Control Number: 2018955253
ISBN 978-1-947506-04-6 (paperback)

Printed in the United States of America
10 9 8 7 6 5 4 3 2 1

First Edition

Cover Design: C. L. Fails

Dedicated to Harriet Kline Hobbs and Stacey Robinson Knoell granddaughter and great-granddaughter of Isaac Franklin Bradley, Sr. in conjunction with the Centennial Anniversary of the Annual Freedom Fund Banquet of the Kansas City, Kansas Branch of the National Association for the Advancement of Colored People NAACP

INTRODUCTION

INTRODUCTION | i

Why now? Better yet, why not now? I have wrestled with both questions lately, and have concluded that now is, indeed, 'the time'.

I am referring to the task of publishing the biography of a distinguished, noteworthy, civil rights leader, who made significant contributions to our country more than one hundred years ago. While America owes a tremendous, invaluable amount of gratitude to Martin Luther King, Jr, Thurgood Marshall, Rosa Parks, and countless other well known legends, whose legacies are widely acknowledged, many lesser celebrated, perhaps unsung heroes, also contributed to the never ending demand for equal justice. One such person was my grandfather, Isaac Franklin Bradley, best known by his initials, I. F. Bradley.

Now, I hesitate to admit that as a rather shy child, I was not overly impressed by, well, actually, much of anything, mainly because I almost apologetically 'perceived' unwarranted attention directed toward me, just because of my last name, alone. And like many children, or in this case, grandchildren, I, therefore, never truly appreciated the enormous contribution that my grandfather gave to humanity. While I do recall having heard many stories about his achievements, particularly from the adults around me during my younger days, I did not fully comprehend the significance of his accomplishments, at that time. Yet, it is now, as I approach the ripe, young, age of seventy-five, that I finally realize the significance of his legacy, and more importantly, the reason that it must be shared with the world.

It was only after I experienced the success of publishing my very first book less than a year ago, that I even entertained the idea of releasing a second book, especially, while I was still in the mood. As a matter of fact, I thought that such a project would prove to be an even easier task than writing the first book, because I had previously compiled most of the material, for my new book, in a speech that I had delivered at a local church. In conjunction with that speech, I prepared a biographical sketch, in the form of a pamphlet, that highlighted milestones in the life of my grandfather.

My first thought, then, was to simply copy that pamphlet. And because it was such a fairly short document of only a very few pages, I thought that the next easiest task would be to just add a copy of the contents of three of his literary works to the final project. What I envisioned as an opportunity to share with scholars of history, a series of documents written by an African American, born over one hundred fifty years ago, turned out to be much more of a challenge than I could ever imagine. Little was I aware of the complications that accompanied such an undertaking. As I encountered one obstacle after another, I nearly gave up on the whole idea.

First of all, I determined that the original copies of each work, that I had planned to simply photocopy, were in such fragile condition, that they would barely be able to withstand the process of copying without further damaging quite a few of the pages. Many of those pages also contained passages that were difficult to read because of age worn print. I then decided to do the next best thing and to simply retype everything.

After I typed the nearly one hundred eighty pages of my chosen documents, I then turned, what I believed to be, my completed manuscript, over to my publisher, who with little hesitation, cautioned me to make sure that I was not violating any copyright laws by attempting to publish something that could possibly be illegal.

I could not imagine that if I did, indeed, have the original copies in my possession, that I could be in danger of violating any law by publishing works by my own grandfather. I did, however, after further research, discover that the works that I had chosen were actually published in 1912 for the first, 1921 for the second, and an undetermined later date for the third. I contacted the copyright office of the Library of Congress and was assured that any works published prior to 1923 automatically fell into public domain. That was great news for at least two of the works. I then decided, 'no problem'. I will simply copy only the first one because it was, after all, the most comprehensive of the three, and I would simply add it to the biographical material, for a completely interesting read.

But then came the kicker. Upon further research at a local library, I was totally shocked to discover that the work that I had chosen to copy titled, *The Reign of Reason*, had already been re-printed by not just one, but by over a half dozen publishers in no fewer than three different languages. As a matter of fact, I found that it can be read in its entirety on the internet, for free. Let me repeat, 'shocked' does not begin to describe my reaction. I also found multiple references to my grandfather on the internet on my home computer, which provided evidence to me that I was not alone in my 'newly' discovered appreciation for the accomplishments of this powerful early twentieth century African American activist.

The next dilemma that became obvious to me, then, was that of determining my true purpose for writing my newly proposed book. Did I really need to reprint something that was already available? Or should I, instead, simply share pertinent information that I had gathered, describing the achievements of a great man, who, over a century ago, against all odds, fought vigorously for equal rights?

vi | REASONS TO **PERSIST**

Because he died six years before my birth, I was not fortunate enough to have known him personally. But when a friend expressed doubt concerning the authenticity of my initial biographical sketch, I realized the importance of citing written documented evidence to verify everything that I wrote, in an effort to avoid the perception that I might be simply writing from hearsay or just memory. In addition to a limited number of written documents that have been passed on to me, some of which include both biographical, as well as, autographical personal passages in his own words, a majority of the evidence that I have found, can be easily accessed on the internet from a variety of websites. My biggest regret, however, is that I did not attempt to address this project earlier in my life, when I could have interviewed people who actually knew my grandfather personally, for the purpose of including their antidotes about him in this work. Any such person would have to have been born nearly one hundred years ago, sometime around 1918, to have been even at least twenty years old at the time of my grandfather's death in 1938. Hence, unfortunately, I know of no one who can now fill that void.

Therefore, I have chosen to craft this work into a narrative that ultimately summarizes data from many fragmented pieces of information, that I have collected from a variety of written sources, into one single document.

While countless books and articles have been written that describe, in detail, multiple important historical events that occurred during his lifetime, I simply, very briefly, only highlight just a very few of them, in an effort to draw attention to the significance of the challenges that Isaac Franklin Bradley encountered throughout his life.

It is my desire, therefore, to share this story with an audience who appreciates the struggles of past generations in their pursuit of justice and equality. It is a story that sets the stage for many questions. In what ways are we facing similar issues today, that our forefather's encountered over one hundred years ago? Do we still have REASONS TO PERSIST? Where do we go from here? Hopefully you will be inspired to examine his trilogy of works, *The Reign of Reason, The Lion and the Lamb,* and *The Truth As To Social Equality, Reason and Common Sense* with the intent of understanding the true essence of motivation that led him to become such a dedicated advocate for the rights of everyone.

As we celebrate the accomplishments of well known, deserving pioneers, on whose shoulders we now stand, we are compelled to also realize that there were many, many individuals who paved the way for the successes that we enjoy today. One such person was Judge, Isaac Franklin Bradley, Sr.

Part One
THE EARLY YEARS

PART ONE: **THE EARLY YEARS | 1**

Isaac Franklin Bradley was born on September 8, 1862 at Hazelwood Hall near Cambridge, in Saline County, Missouri to slave parents, Isaac and Sallie (Davidson) Bradley, only two weeks before Abraham Lincoln released his preliminary Emancipation Proclamation, which the president, subsequently, officially issued just four months later.

Very briefly, the political climate of the nation at the time of his birth was at a highly volatile level. The northern states were in conflict with the southern states in heated competition to dominate the control of power in the Congress. At the heart of the debate was the issue of slavery. While the South vigorously fought for the right to own Negro slaves in an effort to sustain their agricultural economy, Northerners, on the other hand, chose to compare the oppression of slaves to their own oppression by the British, and therefore fought for

2 | REASONS TO PERSIST

the abolition of the institution of slavery.

The Missouri Compromise of 1820 that automatically allowed Missouri to be admitted to the Union as a slave state was challenged by the confrontation known as 'Bleeding Kansas', or 'Border War' that led to the Kansas-Nebraska Act of 1854. While the South needed Kansas to become a slave state, just like it's neighbor, Missouri, The Act allowed Kansans to exercise their right of choice. Outrage in the North, over the Kansas-Nebraska Act spelled the downfall of the old Whig Party, and the birth of the new all-northern Republican Party that fought vigorously to influence Kansans to vote against slavery. Some historians believe that the tension that developed between pro-slavery and anti-slavery forces, that led to the decision of Kansas residents to choose to become a free state, was the final blow that ultimately ignited the spark that marked the beginning of the War Between the States, better known as the Civil War.

It was in the midst of the Civil War, that President Lincoln issued the infamous Emancipation Proclamation, on January 1, 1863, just under four months after the birth of Bradley. The people

PART ONE: THE EARLY YEARS | 3

of Texas, however, did not receive the message until June 19, 1863, which led to the creation of the celebration known as Juneteenth. The proclamation was an executive order that was aimed at the Confederate states in an effort to force them to end their rebellion against the Union. It was designed to abolish slavery, with the Thirteenth Amendment to the Constitution of the United States, as well as to more importantly, preserve the Union. Hence, the politically charged environment under which he was born, significantly influenced the choices that young Bradley ultimately made.

Thus, sets the stage for words that Bradley, himself, printed in the preface to an autobiographical sketch of his early childhood, found in one of his most famous essays titled, *The Reign of Reason*. In it, Bradley states that as the result of 'the criminal practice of slavery that flourished at the time' of his birth, he never saw his father, who left when young Bradley was only about two weeks old.

"I do not remember ever seeing my father, for the reason that very shortly after my

> advent, he took French leave to help settle a little matter of unpleasantness that was on at that time. Missouri was a great place then, especially for hard times, some instances of which I very well remember, among them: That from the time I was about four years old, until I was seventeen, I never had a new hat or a new pair of shoes, in fact, was often short on old ones."

Because public schooling for Colored children was very limited at that time, he received little more than three months of formal education in any one year, for a total of less than eighteen months of schooling altogether, during his youth. Bradley continues:

> "When I was nineteen years old, there came to that little town a man, whose clothes fitted him, and he had manner and bearing altogether different from what I had been accustomed to see, and I learned that he had

> been to the Lincoln Institute in Jefferson City. Up to that time, I had always thought I would try to keep away from that town, however, seeing this man and learning of this new institution, I gathered courage enough to go there."

Thus, inspired by the visitor and determined to obtain a good education, young Bradley saved his earnings, and in 1881, made his way from Cambridge to the Lincoln Institute, a school for the higher education of Negroes, in Jefferson City, Missouri. He persuaded the teachers there to give him an opportunity to work while he attended classes. And after four difficult years of diligent study, he graduated in June, 1885.

During the summer following his graduation, he attempted to write a book, but decided, instead, that he needed to pursue a more professional goal. After much deliberation, he then determined that the field of law presented an excellent opportunity for a young man to succeed in the world. In the fall of that same year, when barriers of racial segregation that existed in most institutions of higher learning in the state of Missouri, excluded students of African descent, he made his way to Lawrence, Kansas, a free state, where he enrolled in the University of Kansas School of Law.

As the only African American in his class, Bradley managed to maintain a very high average rank of ninety-three and one half percent, in spite of overt, as well as, covert racially based obstacles. His persistence paid off, and after just two years of coursework, he graduated in June, 1887 with honors, and a LL.B degree to become the first African American graduate of the KU School of Law.

Soon after graduating from the University of Kansas, Bradley earned permission to practice law in the courts of Kansas, and opened an office in an up-stairs room at 518 Minnesota Avenue in Kansas City.

After just two years in practice, he was elected City Justice of the Peace, Kansas City, Kansas, and served in that position from 1889 to 1891. As the first African American elected judge in the city, he was most frequently addressed by the title, 'Judge' for the remainder of his life.

In 1891, Judge Bradley married Mamie Belle Johnson of Lawrence, Kansas. In an extremely ornate and unusual ceremony that was performed by the Reverend Merritt and witnessed by nearly one hundred eighty invited guests, a Lawrence Daily World newspaper journalist described the occasion as 'the most elaborate event of its kind that ever occurred in Lawrence colored society'. The writer continued:

> 'The bride was attired in a dress of white file francais, made with V-shaped front, short sleeves trimmed with Persian lace, bridal vail, full train, elbow kid gloves, white kid slippers, no jewelry. The walls of the parlor were decorated with flowers. The wedding march was played by the colored mandolin club. The couple received many handsome and costly presents, including articles of furniture, silverware, works of art, ...from their white and colored friends in Lawrence and other cities'.

8 | REASONS TO PERSIST

Shortly after the wedding, the couple moved into their new residence, a large frame house, which Judge Bradley built at 400 Haskell in Kansas City, Kansas, on the edge of Rattlebone Hollow. Rattlebone Hollow included all of the area extending south from the Missouri Pacific tracks to Haskell. It was bounded on the east by 4th Street and on the west by 7th Street. In addition to African Americans, it also was inhabited by German and Slavic immigrants. To that union a daughter, Ruth and son, Isaac Franklin, Jr., were born.

400 Haskell: **Kansas City, Kansas**

Part Two
THE NINETEENTH CENTURY COMES TO AN END

PART TWO: **THE NINETEENTH CENTURY COMES TO AN END | 11**

After serving as City Justice of the Peace, for two years, Judge Bradley returned to private practice until 1894 when he was appointed Deputy County Attorney by Charlie Miller, generally called 'Peg-Leg Miller' because of his one leg. Judge Bradley served in that position until January, 1895, when he became Second Assistant to the County Attorney, and three months later he became the First Assistant, Prosecuting Attorney in Wyandotte County, Kansas, the then most populous and wealthy county in the state, a position that he held until January, 1899.

Although the practice of law was his profession, Judge Bradley took an active leading role in local political and civic affairs. He was an entrepreneur who often teamed with other visionaries in their quest to help organize Negro enterprises in Kansas City, Kansas.

12 | REASONS TO **PERSIST**

One of his earliest business endeavors was the establishment of the American Commercial League Coal and Grain Company. Founded in the early 1890's, the ACL was a joint stock company that dealt in coal, feed, flour, and groceries, that provided basic commodities at reasonable prices, and credit on reasonable terms. Their motto was, 'the best goods, and quickest sales, the smallest profits, and promptest deliveries'. The coal yard was located at 3rd and Minnesota, the grocery outlet at 437 Minnesota, and the main office was located at 402 Minnesota.

Judge Bradley was also an original member of the Afro-American Council, Washington, D. C. of 1898, and later served as a Presidential Elector for the Kansas Republican Party in 1900. During that same year, he joined the Mason, United Brothers of Friendship, Knights of Pythias, where he served as legal counsel for many years.

In a late nineteenth century article titled, *It Happened in Wyandotte*, Judge Bradley offers a personal description of his association with refugees who were part of the Coming of the Exodusters. The Kansas Fever Exodus occurred between 1878 to 1882 at The

PART TWO: **THE NINETEENTH CENTURY COMES TO AN END | 13**

Levee, where many ex-slave refugees, fleeing from the South in pursuit of better living conditions, were brought up the river into Kansas. He recalls:

> "I was a bare headed, bare footed, sparsely clad youngster at Cambridge, a small but important shipping point on the Missouri river, on April 9th, 1879 when the Fannie Lewis, a majestic side wheel steamer, docked at that place. She was towing a couple of great barges upon which was the largest number of refugees that came at any one time. I begged mother to let me go down in the woods to where she landed, and went aboard of her, and heard those mothers and fathers sing and pray and tell some of the story of that from which they had fled. Some of the songs I had heard before, perhaps not sung with the pathos and depth of feeling that I heard that day, and the prayers I heard I can never forget. They sang 'Rock Daniel' and some rocked some as they sang it. They also sang, 'Ride On Jesus, Ride On' and 'I've Done Got Over', and 'Redeemed by the Blood of the Lamb'.

Although he did not sail with the group at that time, Bradley did eventually befriend many of the Exodusters and further elaborated on their journey as follows:

> "All of the refugees did not come on the Fannie Lewis, but the larger portion did. Two other steamers, the Grand Tower and the Durfee, brought cargoes, and others later brought small numbers. They were landed on the low lands south of Jersey Creek and the location was afterwards called Juniper Bottoms. They brought with them the idea of a colony, and had their spiritual adviser in the person of Curtis Pollard, a man of some ability of leadership who, unfortunately did not live long after his arrival. They were close communion Baptists and devout church folks. Dissensions arose and church splits followed, so that out of the mother church which formerly stood at Third and Freeman, there had come King Solomon, Mount Zion, Pleasant Green and Strangers Rest."
>
> The refugees squatted on the river bank

> and built their shacks in irregular form, out of whatever could be pieced together. Industry absorbed them and they gradually bought or built homes in other parts of the city. The guiding hand of the Exodus was Isaiah Montgomery, a full blooded member of our group, and an ex-slave of Jefferson Davis. The number that squatted here was in the neighborhood of five hundred. Montgomery carried a like number to Topeka where they were established in what is still called Tennessee Town. He was also active in planting a colony at Nicodemus in Graham County. Montgomery returned to Mississippi where he later became the owner of the plantation of his former master."

Bradley also noted that most of the nearly twelve thousand colored immigrants, who eventually landed in Wyandotte County, came principally from Tennessee, as well as Louisiana, Alabama, and Mississippi. The numbers were so great, however, that a committee of town people decided to ship a large number of the refugees to other parts of the state including Lawrence, Tonganoxie, Leavenworth, Manhattan, Atchison, Ottawa, in addition to Topeka and Nicodemus.

Consequently, before the turn of the century, when there were not very many Negroes in Kansas City, Kansas, nearly everyone knew everyone else. As a result, most of Judge Bradley's clients, many of whom were Exodusters, also resided in, or near, the West Bottoms, often referred to as "the packing house district", where Saturday night cuttings and shootings in the local saloons and gambling joints occurred far too frequently. While the Reverend George McNeal of the Pleasant Green Baptist Church, located at First and Splitlog, was often called to baptize or to render service to those frequent victims, a physician named Dr. S. H. Thompson, was also called, to treat the wounded.

At that time, Afro-American doctors were not permitted to treat patients in any of the existing hospitals in the city, nor were they able to perform surgery in the average home. Therefore, in 1897, Dr. Thompson, met with Judge Bradley, Dr. H. S. Howell, a physician whose office was located at 1317 North 8th Street, Dr. T. C. Unthank, a physician from

PART TWO: **THE NINETEENTH CENTURY COMES TO AN END | 17**

Kansas City, Missouri, Rev. George McNeal, and the Reverend Calvin Douglass of Western University, to discuss the establishment of a much needed medical facility.

Thus, in May, 1898, the Douglass Hospital, located at 300 Washington Blvd. was founded. While Bradley acknowledged that Dr. Thompson was the driving force behind this initiative, he clarified that the name was chosen, in recognition of the efforts of one of it's founders, the Rev. Calvin Douglass, and not for the abolitionist Frederick Douglass, as many commonly assumed.

Although Judge Bradley was not known to be boastful of his accomplishments, he did enjoy a great sense of pride in the establishment of the new hospital. In the 1900 edition of the University of Kansas Law School senior class magazine, *The Shingle*, he wrote:

> "The Douglass Hospital and Training School for Nurses of which I was one of the founders, and am still the president of the board of directors...is the only thing of the kind in the United States, organized, managed, and

> maintained by Negroes alone and I will add that it is run on the chartable plan and its doors are open to the world, regardless of race, color, or condition."

The hospital later moved to North 27th Street in Quindaro in Kansas City, Kansas.

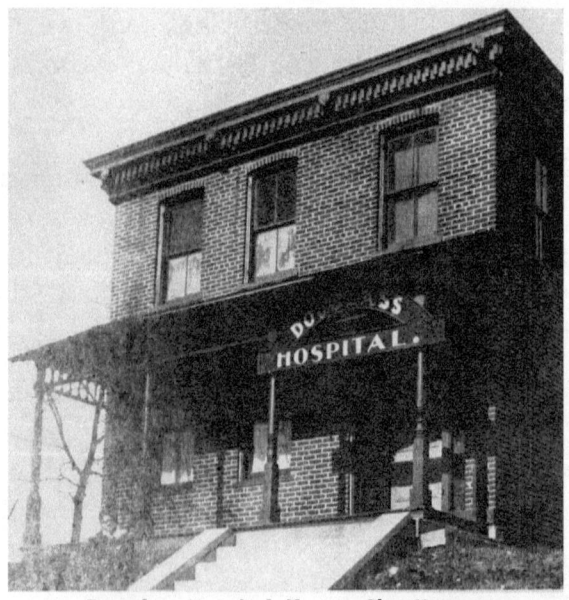

Douglass Hospital: Kansas City, Kansas

Part Three
THE TWENTIETH CENTURY BEGINS

PART THREE: THE TWENTIETH CENTURY BEGINS | 21

At the turn of the twentieth century, a violent revolution overthrew many established Black reconstruction laws, and allowed Jim Crow and legal segregation to become the new law of the land. The Fourteenth Amendment to the Constitution, which, in 1868, had guaranteed full United States citizenship to former slaves, became obsolete. The Fifteenth Amendment that guaranteed the right of suffrage, or the right to vote, to every citizen regardless of race, color, or previous condition of servitude, also became null and void. The response to this national disaster resulted in a complete collapse of the old abolitionist spirit, and led to the emergence of a number of Black leaders, initially the most talented of whom, appeared to be, Booker T. Washington, founder and president of Tuskegee Institute.

While Washington openly disapproved of higher education for Blacks, he also appeared to blame

Blacks for their own plight. One of the most ardent critics of Washington's philosophies was W. E. B. DuBois, a graduate of both Fisk University and Harvard. DuBois strongly opposed nearly all of Washington's policies, especially his attempt to de-value the privileges and the duties of voting, and his opposition to advanced training and higher ambition of the brightest minds. Public reaction to the dispute between Washington and DuBois divided Black American intellectuals into two bitterly antagonistic parties, the Washington Party and the DuBois Party.

It was in the midst of multiple deepening racial crisis, specifically the rising tide of violence where nearly one hundred Black men were reportedly lynched every year, as well as, legal segregation represented by the Supreme Court approval of the 1896 Plessy vs. Ferguson case, which legalized the formula of 'separate, but equal' facilities, and the presence of general voter disenfranchisement, that DuBois met with twenty nine men from thirteen states and the District of Columbia in the vicinity of Buffalo, New York, for the purpose of establishing an organization whose priority would be to aggressively fight for equal rights, and to advocate for higher education of Blacks. Chosen because of its association with the struggle for freedom from slavery as one of the major crossing points on the Underground Railroad for runaway slaves headed to safety in Canada, the men assembled under a tent at Fort Ontario on the Canadian side of Niagara Falls. Thus, the historic meeting became known as The Niagara Movement, and provided for the delegation, a national network for communication and research, that made all Americans aware of the shameful plight of its Black citizens.

The **Niagara Movement**

Among the invited participants to that original group were Judge I. F. Bradley, Sr. and Attorney B. S. Smith, both of whom represented Kansas City, Kansas. The Niagara Movement of 1905 provided the groundwork for the establishment of subsequent civil rights protest organizations, and was the forerunner of the National Association for the Advancement of Colored People, the NAACP.

In 1906, when a proposal for the Commission form of Government for Kansas City, Kansas was introduced and only two cities in the Union had adopted it, the mayor and city council appointed twenty-four men to study, investigate and report on the idea. It was then that John W. West, a liberal Democratic councilman, appointed Judge Bradley to the committee. Judge Bradley, the only African American on the committee, served as a member of the Legal Committee that helped to formally adopt the Commission form of Government for Kansas City, Kansas.

In 1908, Judge Bradley ran for attorney-general for the state of Kansas on the Independence (Hearst) ticket, but subsequently failed to receive enough votes to win. He was successful, however, in organizing the important "Distress Meeting" of 1913, which was the forerunner of the Civic League, of which he was both founder and president. The Civic League was dedicated to improving race relations in the city and was very active in promoting voter registration, as well as, political participation in government. As the result of the efforts of the Civic League, a special statute was passed in 1917 that made it lawful to hire Negroes on the police force of Kansas City, Kansas for the very first time.

In a letter to Attorney General Charles B. Griffith of Kansas, condemning the showing of the Ku Klux Klan sponsored exhibition of "The Birth of a Nation", Judge Bradley wrote on behalf of the Civic League the following:

> "Is there anything that you can do to prevent a presentation, which can do no good: but which may do a great deal of harm? It is a great pity, that men cannot find that, — which better becomes their time and talent, — than this needless appeal to prejudice..."

Similar battles for social justice, became the reasons that many African American leaders refused to compromise, but instead, remained members of the Republican Party to spite the infestation of the Klan in the state at that time. The League continued to strongly advocate for better social and living conditions in the community for many years.

In September 1925, Judge Bradley helped to facilitate a three-year effort to create 'Boy's Day', for the African American youth of Kansas City, Kansas. This unique event focused on an awareness in the community that created the opportunity for nearly twenty-five hundred boys to gather for a huge "Emancipation Celebration" parade, that eventually led to their participation in many other civic activities that addressed racial injustice. "Boy's Week", as well as, "Boy's Day", eventually became an annual feature in the lives of Kansas City youth.

Judge Bradley, in conjunction with his main ally in civic affairs, Dr. S. H. Thompson, as well as, a pharmacist named Frank Davis, also helped to organize the Wyandotte Drug Company located at 1512 North Fifth Street, which later took the name Home Drug Co. This venture addressed a wide range of medical needs in the community and grew to become one of the largest drug stores of its time. The Home Drug Company later became the Gill-Hodges Pharmacy.

Judge Bradley, and Dr. Thompson were also partners with J. W. Jones, Junius Groves and several others in the creation of The Kansas City, Kansas Casket and Embalming Company located at 1014 North 5th Street. Bradley subsequently helped to establish the Mrs. J. W. Jones Funeral Home.

When African American parents living in the North End area of Kansas City, Kansas felt that the journey from Stowe Elementary School, located on 2nd and Virginia, later named Richmond, was too far for their young children to attend, Judge Bradley served as their spokesman in bringing the issue before the then segregated Board of Education, and is recognized as one of the initiators of Dunbar School.

In his constant quest to address the social ills of his community, as well as those of the nation, he was a vigilant, outspoken critic of the government. Judge Bradley expressed his discontent in a trilogy of works, *The Reign of Reason, The Lion and the Lamb,* and *The Truth As To Social Equality, Reason and Common Sense*, that were far advanced from the trends of the time. A unifying theme found in all three works suggests that the difference between what reigns true and what reigns false, is defined by reason and common sense.

The first work, a treatise on political science, titled **The Reign of Reason**, was published in 1912 and copyrighted in 1915. In it he wrote:

> "I have always liked the idea of ascertaining the reason for anything and firmly believed, and still believe, that there is greater power and safety in reason, than there is in any or all things else combined...
>
> ... The truth is, the very soul of that which we think and speak of, as civilization or government, which is also known as the jurisprudence of a people or of an age, is but

> the evolution and application of remedies, to the evils growing out of the system they practice; for the very essence of any law, in the several, and present civilizations, is its remedial force; for where there is no actual wrong, nor any in contemplation, there also, will be an absence of law."

In 1921, he published the second work in the trilogy titled, *The Lion and the Lamb*. In it, he analyzed the law of economics as follows:

> "A system, where the earth would be the common heritage of all who are born therein, for use during life, would be decidedly preferable to a scrambling system wherein it is monopolized and claimed by the inhabitants of any given time; so that all those coming after such time must needs pay some claimant for a place thereon..."

In his the third work titled, *The Truth As To Social Equality, Reason and Common Sense*, he further elaborated on his views about economics, as well as his ideas about social justice. In his introduction to that work, Bradley wrote:

> "Since the formation of the government of the United States, the Negro has been a live and unsolved problem. And in the unsettled condition of world affairs today, it is of increasing proportions. Much has been said in treating this question, but I am inclined to think that more has been said in Mistreatment of it."

Judge Bradley continued his dedication to the importance of the written word by becoming the owner and editor, in 1928, of the *Wyandotte Echo* newspaper. It is interesting to note that many of the early issues of that publication included a section titled 'Things We Believe In', that addressed such concerns as lower taxes, larger industries, more avenues of employment for Negroes, a new senior high school for Negroes, adequate police and fire

PART THREE: **THE TWENTIETH CENTURY BEGINS | 31**

protection, representation in state, county and city offices, and any movement that had the objective of elevating the economic, political and social status of the Negro in America.

Judge Isaac Franklin Bradley, Sr. died on November 8, 1938, after an extended illness, which began in October of 1936. In his service, held on Saturday November 12th at the First African Methodist Episcopal church in Kansas City, Kansas, many leading Negro and white lawyers paid tribute to him, and served as active and honorary pallbearers.

As one of America's leading pioneer African American attorneys, Judge I. F. Bradley, Sr. engaged in a successful practice of law in Kansas City, Kansas for nearly fifty-two years. Against all odds, he worked diligently throughout his life in an effort to create social change that significantly improved the lives of African Americans within his community and beyond. He believed that by applying the principles that he outlined in his three essays, that The Reign of Reason, should enable both The Lion and the Lamb to coexist and to experience The Truth As To Social Equality, (by way of) Reason, and Common Sense. Yes,

Judge Isaac Franklin Bradley, Sr. leaves a legacy that compels future generations to, not merely remember the accomplishments of an outstanding civil rights leader, but to also utilize their talents in the constant effort to demand equality, for there will always be REASONS TO PERSIST.

Judge, **Isaac Franklin Bradley, Sr.**

Reasons to Persist
TIMELINE

TIMELINE: REASONS TO PERSIST | 35

- **1862** — Born to slave parents, Isaac and Sallie (Davidson) Bradley
- **1879** — Boarded the Fannie Lewis Wheel Steamer at the Kansas Fever Exodus
- **1881** — Enrolled in the Lincoln Institute
- **1885** — Graduated from the Lincoln Institute + Enrolled in University of Kansas Law School
- **1887** — First African American Graduate from KU School of Law + Permitted to Practice Law in the Courts of Kansas
- **1889** — Elected Justice of the Peace (1st African American Judge in Kansas City, KS)
- **1890** — Established the American Commercial League Coal & Grain Co.
- **1891** — Married Mamie Belle Johnson
- **1894** — Elected Deputy County Attorney + Served as 2nd Asst. County Attorney & 1st Asst. Prosecuting Attorney, Kansas City, KS
- **1898** — Served as Original Member of the Afro American Council, Washington, D.C. + Founded Douglass Hospital

1900	Served as Presidential Elector for the KS Republican Party + Joined the Masons, United Brothers of Friendship, Knights of Pythias
1905	Became a Charter member of the Niagra Movement
1906	Established the Commission form of Government in Kansas City, KS
1912	Wrote: *The Reign of Reason*
1917	Founded the Civic League of Kansas City
1921	Wrote: *The Lion and the Lamb*
1929	Wrote: *The Truth As To Social Equality, Reason, and Common Sense*
1928	Became Owner and Editor of the *Wyandotte Echo* Newspaper
1938	Died at age 76

REFERENCES

A Brief History of Black Lawyers in Kansas: The Sayers Family

African American Civil Rights: Early Activism and the Niagara Movement; Angela Jones - pp. 156 - 158.

African-American Leaders and Innovators Project - KU Alumni...
www.kualumni.org > Networks & Cubs > Affinity Networks

Blacks in Crimson and Blue - D. M. Davis - American Educational History Journal: Volume 40 #1 & 2 - p. 61 - http://books.google.com/books?isbn=1623964237

Bradley, Isaac F., 1862-1938. - *Social Networks and Archival Context* - SNAC snaccooperative.org/ark:/99166/w6vb1t1s

Critique of Poets - The Limits of Art - A. R. Biswas - p. 375

Ebony Magazine: Great Moments in Black History, No. VII - THE NIAGARA

MOVEMENT: - May 1976; https://
books.google.com/books/about/Ebony.
html?id=2t8DAAAAMBAJ; p. 134

I.F. Bradley, Sr. family papers, 1976 - The
University of Kansas
text.ku.edu/view?docld=ksrlead/ksrl.
kc.bradleyifsr.xml;route=ksrlead;brand..

Greater Kansas City and the Urban Crisis, 1830-
1968; Van William Hutchison; An Abstract of a
Dissertation - p. 105

Negro Statistical Bulletin - Issues 1 - 17 - Page 4 -
Google Books Result - p. 4
http://books.google.com/
books?id=zK1NAQAAMAAJ

*The History of Our Public Schools Wyandotte
County, Kansas* - Juniper - Kansas City, Kansas
Public Schools; Patricia Adams - www.kckps.org/
disthistory/areahistory/juniper.htm

The Ku Klux Klan in Kansas City, Kansas 1921-1930;
An Abstract of the Thesis of Timothy D. Rives - p.
75.

REFERENCES | 41

The Pittsburg Courier from Pittsburg, Pennsylvania
- November 1938 - p. 21
https://www.newspapers.com/newspage/40093452/

The Reign of Reason - I. F. Bradley

African American Jayhawks Make A Difference

Dedication of Buildings and Burning Mortgages of The Bishop Williams School of Religion and Douglas Hospital Western University at Kansas City, Kansas ; June 3, 1943: p. 3

KU LAW Magazine for Alumni and Friends - Fall 2015 - p. 11

The Afro-American Community in Kansas City, Kansas - 1980; 1982: pp. 86, 88, 89, 92, 93, 95, 109

The Lion and the Lamb - I. F. Bradley

The Truth As To Social Equality, Reason and Common Sense - I. F. Bradley

The Rise and Fall of Western University; Orrin McKinley Murray, Sr.; February 29, 1960; p. 17

The University of Kansas: KU Law Magazine - Spring 2004 p.3 & p.34

Who's Who in Colored America - A Biographical Dictionary of Notable Living Persons of African Descent in America - 1927: pp. 53-54

Who's Who in Colored America - A Biographical Dictionary of Notable Living Persons of African Descent in America - 1928 - 1929; p22

It Happened in Wyandotte; Written notes by I. F. Bradley, Jr.

Lawrence Daily World: 1891

Personages of the Afro-American Race; p 579

Progress of a Race: The Remarkable Advancement of the Afro-American - From the Bondage of Slavery, Ignorance and Poverty to the Freedom of Citizenship, Intelligence, Affluence, Honor and Trust - 1901

The Shingle - published by the Senior Class of the Kansas University Law School -1900 - Kansas State

REFERENCES | 43

Historical Society

The Wyandotte Echo - Vol. I, No 12; p. 1

Biography of the Twenty-Seven; p. 30

African American Physician Trailblazers Honoring Our Past

The Kansas City Kansan from Kansas City, Kansas on November 15…
https://www.newspapers.com/newspage/59594419/

The Kansas City Kansan from Kansas City, Kansas on September 17…
https://www.newspapers.com/newspage/59689859/

Kansas Ethnic Council, Inc. Ethnic History of Wyandotte County. vol. 1. Kansas City: Kansas City, Kansas Ethnic Council, n.d.

The Kansas City Gazette from Kansas City, Kansas: September 13
http://www.newspapers.com/newspage/61576015/

Black History Month; African American legal

Pioneer - Kansas Bar...
www.ksbar.org/blogpost/1106646/LOMAP-Tech-Tips?tag=Black+History

The Educational Experiences of Ex-Slaves at the University of Kansas from the 1870s - 1920s; Donna M. Davis

EPILOGUE

EPILOGUE | 47

Isaac Franklin Bradley, Jr., son of Judge Isaac Franklin Bradley, Sr., continued the legacy of his father's REASONS TO PERSIST, as a respected attorney in Kansas City, Kansas. He, too, was best known by his initials, I. F.

I. F. Bradley, Jr. was born on February 13, 1895 in Kansas City, Kansas. The family lived in the northeast section of the city, on the corner of Fourth Street and Haskell Avenue, where young Bradley and his sister, Ruth, enjoyed such luxuries as Shetland ponies and a buggy, in which they rode around town with hordes of children following them. He attended private schools before graduating from Sumner High School in 1912. In 1917, he graduated from the University of Kansas School of Law, the alma-mater of his father.

48 | REASONS TO PERSIST

2nd Lieutenant: **Isaac Franklin Bradley, Jr.**

EPILOGUE | 49

Soon after he received his degree from KU, I. F. Bradley, Jr. volunteered to enter military service. As a veteran of two wars, he joined the United States Army during World War I, and was sent to the Officers Training School in Des Moines, Iowa, and later to the Officer's Training School at Camp Pike, Arkansas where in 1918 he was commissioned 2nd Lieutenant of Infantry. During World War II, he was commissioned Captain of the first Separate Company of African American men in the newly formed Kansas State Guard, which was organized as a replacement for the Kansas National Guard that had been called to active duty.

In 1931, he married Gladys Graham of Des Moines, Iowa. Soon after the wedding, the couple moved into their new residence on the corner of Twelfth Street and Everett Avenue in Kansas City, Kansas.

In addition to experiencing a lucrative law practice, with his law partner, Judge A. B. Howard, Attorney I. F. Bradley, Jr. served as Special Assistant to the Attorney General of Kansas under Jay S. Parker, and in the same capacity, under Attorney General Mitchell during the 1930's. He was also registered to practice in the Kansas Supreme Court. In 1946, he was appointed attorney and counselor of the United States Circuit Court of Appeals for the Tenth Circuit. He was a long time member of both the Wyandotte County Bar Association and the Kansas City, Kansas Bar Association.

As a member of several civic and social organizations, Attorney Bradley was especially proud of his affiliation with the Alpha Phi Alpha Fraternity, Inc. He was active in the preliminary work for establishing the Upsilon Chapter at the University of Kansas in Lawrence, and was a charter member of that chapter. He was also a charter member of Beta Lambda Chapter of Alpha Phi Alpha in Greater Kansas City.

He was a charter member of Progress Lodge No. 77 of the Masonic Lodge. In 1956, he served as Commander of the American Legion, as well as the Legion of Guardsmen. He also belonged to the Trouveur Club of Kansas City, Kansas, and the 40 Years Ago Column Club.

During the civil rights movement of the nineteen sixties, Attorney I. F. Bradley, Jr. rose to the occasion that inspired him to join the nation, in numerous sit-ins and protest marches, while at the same time, he diligently fought for social justice in the courts of the state of Kansas.

Attorney Bradley was a Trustee of the First African Methodist Episcopal Church of Kansas City, Kansas, where he was also an active member of the Silent Crusaders Club.

In a personal memoir, I. F. Bradley, Jr. declared that he had no hobbies because it took "up too much time." He did note, however, that he had "looked out on the Pacific and on the Atlantic (from land)", as well as, "looked over into Canada (from U. S. soil)". On a personal note, I might add that I do recall that he refused to ever board an airplane.

He died in 1975 after fifty-six years in the practice of law. Cherished by two daughters, Frances Bradley Robinson and Harriet Kline Hobbs, Attorney Isaac Franklin Bradley, Jr. leaves a legacy of social activism that did indeed improve the lives of African Americans in Kansas City, Kansas, for he, too, like his father, understood the power of **REASONS TO PERSIST.**

APPENDIX

The Reign of Reason.

A Treatise on Political Economy ::

By I. F. Bradley

Price 50 Cents

APPENDIX | 57

Mamie Belle **Johnson Bradley**

APPENDIX | 59

Ruth and Isaac Franklin Bradley, Jr. with Shetland Ponies and Carriage

BETA LAMBDA CHAPTER
Upper—left to right—Dr. Pyles, Dr. Lee, Dr. A. O. Mitchell, Attorney R. H. Gillum.
Lower—Dr. Norwood, Rev. Isaacs, Prof. Morrison, Prof.
W. R. Howell, Atty. I. F. Bradley, Jr.

APPENDIX | 61

Attorney **I. F. Bradley, Jr.**

ABOUT THE AUTHOR

ABOUT THE AUTHOR

Frances Bradley Robinson at 1964 Civil Rights Demonstration

Frances Bradley Robinson is a retired music teacher, who has a legacy of community service in Kansas, Missouri, Nebraska, and Iowa. She is a third generation graduate of the University of Kansas, and holds Life Memberships in both the National Association for the Advancement of Colored People and Alpha Kappa Alpha Sorority, Inc. While she currently serves as Minister of Music at her church, she is especially proud of her daughter, a newly elected political official, who now represents a new generation of activists, who realize that there will always be REASONS TO **PERSIST**.

Stacey Robinson Knoell with mother
Frances Bradley Robinson at 2017 Women's March Demonstration

www.ingramcontent.com/pod-product-compliance
Lightning Source LLC
Chambersburg PA
CBHW030101100526
44591CB00008B/227